Magical Places

of Britain

MAGICAL PLACES OF BRITAIN by Rob Wildwood 2013

Photography, text, layout and design by Rob Wildwood

All photos, text and graphics in this book are subject to copyright
© 2013 Rob Wildwood

Text in italics is quoted from folklore and other publicly available sources.

First published in 2013
Second edition printed 2014

Wyldwood Publishing, Tower House, York, YO10 4UA, UK

Printed by Gutenberg Press, Malta

ISBN 978-0-9575433-0-0

Front cover: Janet's Foss, a magical waterfall in North Yorkshire inhabited by a fairy.
Front flap: Ancient chestnut tree in Roslin Glen, Scotland.
Back cover: Stream running by the old mill in Mulgrave Woods, Yorkshire.
Back flap: Pistyll Rhaeadr Waterfall, Wales.
Opposite: A tree spirit carved into a tree on Dundon Beacon, Somerset.
Overleaf, left: Part of the ruined walls of Castell Dinas Bran in Wales.
Overleaf, right: Sea caves by Tintagel Haven, Cornwall.

Magical places of Britain

By Rob Wildwood

Three years ago I embarked upon a quest that would take me to some of Britain's most magical places...

"It all began in Merlin's Cave in Tintagel where I had a vision of the wizard Merlin initiating me into his magic circle. From there I was guided to visit other magical places and soon found myself on the slopes of the sacred mountain of Schiehallion in Scotland, the 'Fairy Hill of the Caledonians'. There I had a vision of the fairy queen Maeve who told me that I should not keep my discoveries secret but should publish them and reveal them to the world...

I had no idea how to do this but after a year of visiting sacred sites and magical places I knew I had to get the information out there somehow. I started by publishing a blog called The Land of the Fae at www.landofthefae.com where I posted photos and talked about the magical experiences I had in these places, including extracts of local folklore.

It was another year before I decided that I should compile a book of my travels. By that time I had undertaken extensive research and visited and photographed dozens of magical places, some of which were well known, while others were remote, hidden or forgotten.

This book is the result of all that work and my three years of explorations around the British Isles. By publishing this book I hope to bring these hidden places back to life, and to raise awareness of our magical landscape and make people realize that magic does still exist, even in our modern world, it did not die out with the onset of the modern age but is still out there waiting to be rediscovered, and waiting for the day when people will once again understand the power of these sacred locations.

My hope is that these special places will continue to be treated with the respect and reverence that they deserve as places of sanctity."

Rob Wildwood

how to find a magical place

At the end of each section you will find a list of directions to each of the Magical Places. Using these directions you will be able to find these places using either a map or the internet.

When using a map, search for the place name first (in italics e.g. *Poolewe, Highland*) and then follow our written instructions from there. Finding the exact location will be made easier if you can get hold of a local 1:25 000 scale OS (Ordnance Survey) Explorer Map. These are usually available in local newsagents near the location which you want to explore, or can be ordered online beforehand.

Using the internet it is much easier to pinpoint the exact location. You will need to go to a website which can display OS (Ordnance Survey) maps (Currently these can be viewed at www.streetmap.co.uk or www.bing.com). At www.streetmap.co.uk you can either enter the map coordinates directly (e.g. NG778897) or you can search for the place name and follow our written instructions from there. If you enter the map coordinates directly then zoom out to view the local 1:25 000 scale OS map. If you enter the place name then you will have to zoom in to view this map. (Note that some places are tagged as "unmarked" in our directions which means that the exact location is not indicated on the 1:25 000 scale OS maps, in which case you will have to use our directions to find the exact location).

Rights of Way

In Scotland you have the 'right to roam', which means that you are allowed to walk almost anywhere so long as you are not in someone's private garden or yard. In England and Wales you are restricted to public footpaths and open access land (as indicated on the OS maps). To enter areas with no right of public access you should contact the landowner for permission first. Areas with no public access will say "seek permission first" in our Directions section.

The island of Albion

In ancient times the island of Britain was ruled by wild magic and elemental spirits of nature. Arthur and his knights roamed the land, faery magic haunted the twilight and the wild hunt could be heard crashing through the skies at night. This was the magical island of Albion, a legendary isle at the edge of the known World, the sacred island of Merlin the wizard.

There were once many places in Britain where the ancient magic of this isle could still be felt. But now, due to the ravages of time and the relentless onslaught of civilization, only a handful of these places still survive. Having escaped centuries of change these sacred places have become all but forgotten, little pockets of wild magic in a modern landscape.

In these magical places the ancient magic can still sometimes be felt and experienced if one is only willing to pause there for a while and let the clutter of the modern world recede from our minds to be replaced by the stillness of nature and the echoes of our ancient past.

In this book we shall explore these magical locations and shed some light upon these enchanted corners of our land that have lain shrouded in darkness and mystery for so long...

Left: The Fairy Cross Plain, North Yorkshire. *Right:* Longaford Tor, above Wistman's Wood on Dartmoor, Devon.

Contents

Enchanted Forests

The Ancient Wildwood that once covered the whole of the British Isles fell long ago to the woodsman's axe, but in a few isolated locations you may still find remnants of this ancient forest.

In these places you will be taken back to a time when the land was ruled by wild spirits of nature and haunted by faery magic. Only in the deep forest, far from civilization is this connection to the spirits of the ancient wildwood still possible.

Hidden dells and secluded glens that have escaped the ravages of time are small pools of ancient magic in a modern landscape.

1. **Coille Loch an Draing, Highland**
    The haunt of the friendly Gairloch Fairy

2. **The Fairy Dell, Yorkshire**
    A small enchanted fairy dell

3. **Dundon Beacon, Somerset**
    A natural temple and a sacred tree spirit

4. **Mulgrave Woods, Yorkshire**
    Home of the wicked fairy Jeanie o' Biggersdale

5. **The Fairy Glen, Conwy**
    An enchanted wooded valley

6. **Roslin Glen, Midlothian**
    Hidden beneath the mysterious Rosslyn Chapel lies a deeper mystery

7. **Tarn Hole, Yorkshire**
    A hidden valley on the moors that was home to a hob

8. **The New Forest, Hampshire**
    A pixie haunted forest where young ponies are lured into the swamps

9. **Goblin Combe, Somerset**
    A bunch of primroses opens a gateway to the fairy realm

10. **Wistman's Wood, Devon**
    An ancient twisted oakwood on Dartmoor where the wild hunt rides

Enchanted Forests

1. Coille Loch an Draing

Gairloch, Highland

Gille **D**ubh the **G**airloch **F**airy used to haunt these woods. **H**e was described as having black hair and wearing clothes of leaves and moss. **H**e was a kind and helpful spirit but despite this local chieftains decided to hunt him down. **T**hey searched the whole forest and were unable to find him but since that day he has never been seen again.

Previous pages and this page: The enchanted forest of
Coille Loch an Draing.

2. The Fairy Dell

Denton, Ilkley, Yorkshire

A hidden valley near Ilkley in Yorkshire that is haunted by the Fairy Folk.

Main: A hidden waterfall in the Fairy Dell

3. Dundon Beacon

Compton Dundon, Somerset

Dundon Beacon, together with Lollover Hill, forms the Gemini in the Glastonbury landscape zodiac. The whole hill is a nature reserve, with wooded flanks and a large clearing on the summit which forms the interior of a large Iron Age hillfort. In springtime the wooded flanks are full of bluebells and ramsons, while in summer the grassy summit is carpeted with wild buttercups and orchids.

A small clearing on the Northeastern side of the hill has a sacred spring and the carved face of a tree spirit in a large horse chestnut tree. People from the surrounding area sometimes gather here to perform small ceremonies and leave offerings.

Left: The face of a tree spirit carved into one of the horse chestnut trees. *Above*: Sacred spring on the side of Dundon Beacon. *Opposite*: Two large horse chestnut trees create a natural temple.

4. Mulgrave Woods

&

Jeannie the Fairy

Sandsend, Yorkshire

Mulgrave **W**oods is an extensive area of woodland covering several gorges and a broad river valley in **N**orth **Y**orkshire. **O**n an eminence in the centre of the forest stands the ruin of a 12th century **N**orman castle, while deeper in the woods lies an even more ancient fortification, a mound said to have been built by the giant **W**ade in the 6th century. **A** side gorge known as the **W**izard's **G**len hides a high waterfall which falls into a deep gully known as **B**iggersdale **H**ole, while near the head of the main valley lies an old ruined millhouse which featured in the 19th century novel **J**eanie o' **B**iggersdale. **T**he novel was based upon earlier folklore about a wicked fairy who was said to haunt these woods:

"A very mischievous fairy, Jeanie of Biggersdale, resided at a place so called at the head of Mulgrave woods. A bold young farmer, perhaps under the influence of John Barleycorn, undertook one night, on a wager, to approach the habitation of this sprite, and to call her : but his rashness nearly cost him his life ; Jeanie angrily replied that she was coming, and while he was escaping across the running stream, he fared worse than Burns's Tarn O'Shanter, when pursued by Nanny the witch ; for Jeanie overtaking him just as his horse was half across, cut it in two parts though fortunately he was on the half that got beyond the stream!"

Jeanie the fairy was said to live in a cave near **F**oss **C**astle called **H**ob **C**ave.

Left: Barnby Beck, one of several streams running through the mysterious Mulgrave Woods. *Above*: Hidden away in the centre of the forest you will find the medieval Mulgrave Castle.

This page: A large rock basin sits in a magical location in the centre of the stream near the old millhouse in Mulgrave Woods. *Far left:* The waterfall in Biggersdale Hole. *Left above:* Stream flowing out of the Wizard's Glen. *Left below:* An old shrine hidden away in Mulgrave Woods above the Wizard's Glen.

5. The Fairy Glen

Betws-y-Coed, Conwy

The river Conwy flows through the beautiful Fairy Glen, a secluded gorge containing an ancient remnant of enchanted woodland.

Many fairy sightings have been recorded in the local area.

Left: The enchanted Fairy Glen near Conwy Falls. *Above*: The river Conwy flowing through the Fairy Glen. *Right*: The Afon Machno flowing into the river Conwy just above Conwy Falls.

6. Roslin Glen

Roslin, Midlothian

Below the mysterious Rosslyn chapel, famous for it's strange Knights Templar symbology and appearance in the Da Vinci Code novel lies the even more mysterious Roslin Glen.

This primeval woodland lies in a steep gorge shrouded in mystery. There are strange stone carvings, holy wells, smugglers' caves and some truly ancient trees.

Curious pathways wind down the side of the gorge and follow the banks of the river, while in places huge old trees form natural temples of pagan worship in forest clearings.

Roslin Castle also overlooks the glen and is haunted by a ghost dog, a white lady and a black knight.

Wallace's Cave on the opposite side of the gorge is a challenge to reach. It was said to be a hideout of the famous William Wallace while he was on the run from English soldiers. Around the cave can be found more mysterious rock carvings.

Far left and right: Ancient chestnut trees growing in Roslin Glen. *Left:* Gargoyle on Rosslyn Chapel. *Top:* A strange face carved into the rock. *Middle:* Yew trees forming part of a 'yew circle'. *Bottom*: The North Esk River flowing through Roslin Glen.

7. Tarn Hole

Bilsdale, North Yorkshire

A magical hidden woodland in a remote part of the North York Moors that is home to a small, shaggy spirit known as a Hob.

The North York Moors abounds with such hidden gullies containing small remnants of ancient woodland.

Main: Tarn Hole Beck flows out of Tarn Hole through a patchwork quilt of autumn leaves.

8. The New Forest

Minstead, Hampshire

The New Forest in Hampshire abounds with tales of the pixies which haunt it's mysterious glades. **In the 1920's there** were seen:

"several little people who climbed the trees of the forest, possessing catlike attributes for better balance".

Also spirits known as "colt-pixies" would lure young ponies to their deaths in the marshy parts of the heath.

Main: A carpet of bluebells in a spring g
New Forest

9. Goblin Combe

Cleeve, Somerset

A girl out collecting primroses in Goblin Combe accidentally dropped them on a rock and opened a gate to Fairyland. The Fairies liked the primroses so they gave her a golden ball. Later a boy tried to copy her hoping for a similar gift, but this time the Fairies were angry with his greed and swept him away to Faeryland and neither he nor the gateway was ever seen again.

On a hill overlooking Goblin Combe known as Cleeve Toot the Druids once performed magical rituals.

10. Wistman's Wood

Dartmoor, Devon

This ancient forest of tangled oak trees is home to the legendary whist hounds, a pack of spectral black dogs with blood red fangs. They issue forth from the forest at night with their master Old Crockern who leads the Wild Hunt.

No one knows the true age of this ancient forest who's haunted depths are kept protected by dark spirits and adder infested boulders.

Previous page: The twisted and knarled depths of Wistman's Wood.
This page: A strange tree shaped like a troll in Wistman's Wood.
Offerings to the spirits of the forest are left in his outstretched hand.

Directions to the Enchanted Forests & Glens

1. Coille Loch an Draing
Poolewe, Highland
Follow the B8057 North from Poolewe to Midtown. Take the left hand turning just after the second church in Midtown and follow it until it turns into a track. Then continue walking for about 4 miles until you reach Loch an Draing which will be the third loch you come to - NG778897

2. Fairy Dell
Denton, North Yorkshire
Follow the lane Northwest out of Denton and turn left when you reach a fork in the road at Lane End Farm. Continue down this lane for about a mile until you reach the end at Hollingley Farm, then follow a public footpath to the left that leads down into the Fairy Dell - SE126509

3. Dundon Beacon
Compton Dundon, Somerset
From the village of Dundon take the small lane that leads past the school, and when you reach the end turn right into the nature reserve. The clearing with the spring lies at the end of a small track that leads off to the left partway up the hill - ST485323

4. Mulgrave Woods
Sandsend, North Yorkshire
Mulgrave woods lies on a private estate but is open the public on Wednesdays and weekends and can be accessed from the village of Sandsend, north of Whitby. Mulgrave Castle - NZ839116. Biggersdale Hole - NZ839112. The old mill - NZ830116.

5. The Fairy Glen
Betws-y-coed, Conwy
A couple of miles South of Betws-y-coed on the A5 there is a car park for visitors to Conwy Falls by the B4406 to Penmachno. A small entrance fee is payable there where you can walk down winding paths to the falls and the Fairy Glen - SH809534

6. Roslin Glen
Roslin, Midlothian
Head Southeast from the village of Roslin to Rosslyn Chapel. Continue down the lane that passes to the left of the chapel until you come to a private driveway ahead. The path down into Roslin Glen then forks off to the right through the trees. You will see that ancient chestnut tress away to your left as you walk down - NT279632

7. Tarn Hole
Chop Gate, North Yorkshire
Park in Bilsdale near The Grange and follow public footpaths Notheastwards up towards the moor and Tarn Hole. Seek permission of the landowner to explore further - SE589975

8. The New Forest
Minstead, Hampshire
The New Forest covers a huge area Southwest of Minstead. A fairy mound called Cold Pixie's Cave can be found at SU349016

9. Goblin Combe
Cleeve, Somerset
Take Cleeve Hill Road south out of Cleeve and park in the car park opposite the church. Follow the public footpath North and East towards Cleeve Toot and continue for about 2km through the Goblin Combe. Cleeve Toot is at ST462655

10. Wistman's Wood
Two Bridges, Devon
Take the public footpath North out of Two Bridges following the East bank of the river for about 2km until you reach Wistman's Wood - SX612772

Haunted Waters

Lakes, pools and waterfalls were often haunted by female water spirits such as Nymphs or Jennies. These seductive female spirits could lure unwary travellers and drown them in their hidden depths.

Other waters have strange tales and legends associated with them, stories of drowned villages, magical fish and fairy hauntings.

These sacred places have an eerie sense of timelessness about them, as the eternal forces of nature constantly recycle and replenish the ever-flowing water.

Magical Pools & Waterfalls

11. Janet's Foss

Malham, North Yorkshire

One of the most magical places in the British Isles, the fairy queen Janet is is said to live in a hidden cave behind the waterfall.

Previous pages: Janet's Foss. *This page*: The enchanted waterfall, pool and cave. The entrance to Janet's cave is to the right of the waterfall near the top. To the far right of the picture is another unrelated cave. *Inset*: The entrance to Janet's cave. If you manage to make it down the treacherous path from the top of the waterfall to the entrance, crawl right to the end of the cave and speak into the hole above you, your voice will resonate deeply through hidden caverns behind the waterfall.

12. St. Nectan's Glen

Tintagel, Cornwall

A place of healing and pilgrimage set in a magical wooded valley. Folk travel here from far and wide to leave offerings and receive healing and visions. Many strange phenomena have been recorded in this magical spot where the water cascades through a narrow gorge known as St. Nectan's Kieve.

Nechtain was a Celtic water deity who later became Christianised as St. Nectan. The saint's sanctuary and hermitage are located near to the fall.

Previous page left: Water cascades through a magical portal which some say is an entrance to the Otherworld.

Previous page inset: Offerings left tied to a bush in St. Nectan's Kieve for healing and wishes.

Previous page main: Coins hammered into a money tree in St. Nectan's Kieve.

Right: The waterfall plunges 30 ft into a large stone basin, before swirling around and emerging through a circular hole into a shallow tranquil pool. St. Nectan's silver bell is said to lie hidden in the stone basin, while the breath of the water god Nechtain can be seen issuing forth from the stone hole. Millions of years of erosion have created a series of bowl shaped grooves around the edge of this fall.

Opposite: The outflow of water from St. Nectan's Kieve. Pilgrims pile rocks here into towers and leave ribbons tied to the trees.

Above: The magical woodlands of St. Nectan's Glen.

13. Pistyll Rhaeadr

Tan-y-pistyll, Powys

One of the tallest waterfalls in Wales and certainly one of the the most magical!

The falls are in three parts, the tall upper fall, the short middle fall that drops through the Fairy Bridge, and the lower fall which drops into a pool at the head of the Afon Rhaeadr river.

Locals say that the natural arch called the Fairy Bridge is used by the fairies hidden in the moss-green banks to cross from one side to the other.

The falls are haunted by two spirits, that of a white lady and that of a monk. The white lady can be seen in the tallest fall with her long hair draped in front of her face, while the monk in his long robes guards the lower falls.

In the rocks above the upper fall there once lived a winged serpent who would cool himself in the fast flowing waters and feast upon his prey there, and sometimes the waters would flow red with the blood of his victims.

The serpent, known as a Gwiber, was eventually killed by being enticed to attack a red-cloaked pillar covered in spikes.

Left: Water flows under the fairy bridge down to the lower falls. *Inset top:* The upper falls. *Inset middle*: The falls sit at the head of a narrow valley and create the Afon Rhaeadr river. *Inset bottom*: The Fairy Bridge. *Far right:* The upper and lower falls.

14. Llyn y Fan Fach

Llanddeusant, Carmarthenshire

A fairy maiden once lived in this lake and was wooed by a local farmer who had to bake her some perfect bread. He eventually succeeded and they had several children together, but after he accidentally struck her for the third time she fled and returned to the lake with all her fairy cattle and wealth.

She still came back occasionally to teach her sons about herbs and medicine, and with all this knowledge they became famous doctors known as the Physicians of Myddfai as attested to in ancient Welsh manuscripts.

Main: Llyn y Fan Fach sits high in the Welsh hills surrounded by towering mountains.

15. The Fairy Lochs

Badachro, Highland

The Fairy Lochs lie to the south of Sithean Mor "The Large Fairy Mound".

Tales of the Sidhe, or fairy folk, abound in this remote area of Scotland.

Main: Sithean Mor "The Large Fairy Mound" overlooks the Northernmost of the Fairy Lochs "Lochan Sgeireach".

16. The Queen of Fairies' Island

Loch Maree, Highland

In a remote corner of Scotland there is a large loch called Loch Maree and on that loch there is a large island called Eilean Subhainn. Within that island there is another small hidden loch, and on that loch there is another tiny island! An island within an island within an island! A legendary place where on certain nights of the year the Queen of the Fairies is said to hold court.

Main: The Queen of Fairies Island sits in a lake on the island of Eilean Subhainn, which itself sits in the much larger lake known as Loch Maree.

17. Wharton Tarn

Hawkshead Hill, Cumbria

Reputed to be the haunt of fairies this mysterious lake is also inhabited by **J**enny **G**reenteeth, the water hag of local legend. **W**ith green skin, long lank hair and sharp teeth this terrifying spirit would drag young and old into the water to drown.

Main: Wharton Tarn is also known as Jenny Greenteeth's Tarn. Don't wander too close to edge or Jenny may leap out and drag you in!

18. Keld Head Spring

Pickering, North Yorkshire

This powerful spring produces thousands of gallons of crystal clear water every day which bubbles up through sandy beds at the bottom of the pool.

In ancient times the legendary King Peredurus was said to have lost his valuable golden ring while swimming in this spring. After much fruitless searching the ring was discovered years later in the belly of a pike on his banqueting table!

Main and inset bottom: The outflow from Keld Head Spring. *Inset top:* Spring water bubbling up through the sandy beds of Keld Head Spring.

19. Lake Gormire

Sutton Bank, North Yorkshire

This lake was said be created when a cataclysmic earthquake drowned a whole village. The church bells can still sometimes be heard ringing eerily from beneath the surface of the lake while those compelled to swim the lake have sworn they see chimneys and rooftops far below.

The lake is also said to be bottomless and a local legend tells of how a goose was once sucked into its depths only to re-emerge miles away stripped of all its feathers!

A local saying prophesies:

'When Gormire riggs shall be covered with hay, The White Mare of Whitestonecliff will bear it away.'

Above: The crystal clear water of Lake Gormire completely freezes over in winter time. *Right*: The ancient woodland surrounding Lake Gormire takes on the russet hues of autumn.

20. The Fairy's Hole

Swaledale, Yorkshire

A hidden cave behind a waterfall that leads to the land of faerie.

Left: Summer Lodge Beck emerges from underground caverns.
Above: The waterfall which flows into the fairies' pool. Behind the waterfall is the tiny entrance to a cave system where with the right equipment you can climb down the fairies' hole into an underground realm.

Directions to Enchanted Waterfalls & Pools

11. Janet's Foss
Malham, North Yorkshire
Take the road East out of Malham and after about 1km there is a public footpath on the right which leads down to Janet's Foss - SD911632

12. St. Nectan's Glen
Halgabron, Cornwall
The entrance to St. Nectan's Glen is on the main road about a mile East of Tintagel near the village of Trethevey. Follow the footpath through the narrow wooded gorge until you reach the cafe above St. Nectan's Kieve. An entrance fee is then payable to walk down to the waterfall - SX080885

13. Pistyll Rhaeadr
Llanrhaeadr-ym-Mochant, Powys
Take the road heading Northwest out of Llanrhaeadr-ym-Mochant up the valley of the Afon Rhaeadr until you reach the very end (after about 6km) where there is a small car park and a cafe. The falls are directly ahead of you with several paths leading up and around the falls - SJ071295

14. Llyn y Fan Fach
Llandduesant, Carmarthenshire
Head East out of Llanduesant until you reach the car park at the end of the road. Continue over the bridge on foot and after about 2km you will reach the lake - SN802218

15. The Fairy Lochs
Badachro, Highland
From Badachro head East to Shieldaig. Take the track that heads Southwest from Shieldaig Farm and follow the footpath that fork off to the left, heading uphill all the time. After about 1km you will come to the first of the Fairy Lochs marked on the map as Lochan Sgeireach - NG810713

16. Queen of Fairies Island
Loch Maree, Highland
Drive along the A832 which runs South of Loch Maree and stop at the Loch Maree Hotel in Talladale. There you should be able to hire a boat to take you over to the island of Eilean Subhainn - NG923720

17. Wharton Tarn
Hawkshead Hill, Cumbria
Head West out of Hawkshead Hill until you reach the first road junction. Follow the public footpath heading North from there until you see the tarn on your left - SD331987

18. Keld Head Spring
Pickering, North Yorkshire.
Keld Head Spring is by the main road going West out of Pickering, just south of the A170 between Street Lane and Westgate Carr Road - SE787844

19. Lake Gormire
Sutton Bank, North Yorkshire
Park at the Sutton Bank National Park Centre and head West until you reach Sutton Bank. Follow the footpath Northwest along Sutton Brow and take the first path to the left that leads down the scars through Garbutt Wood to Lake Gormire - SE503832

20. The Fairies' Hole
Summer Lodge, North Yorkshire
Follow the B6270 West until you pass Feetham. Turn left towards Crackpot and continue until you reach the end of the tarmac. Keep going up the track until you reach the head of the valley and then take a small unmarked path which leads left down a steep muddy path towards the fairies' hole - SD963952

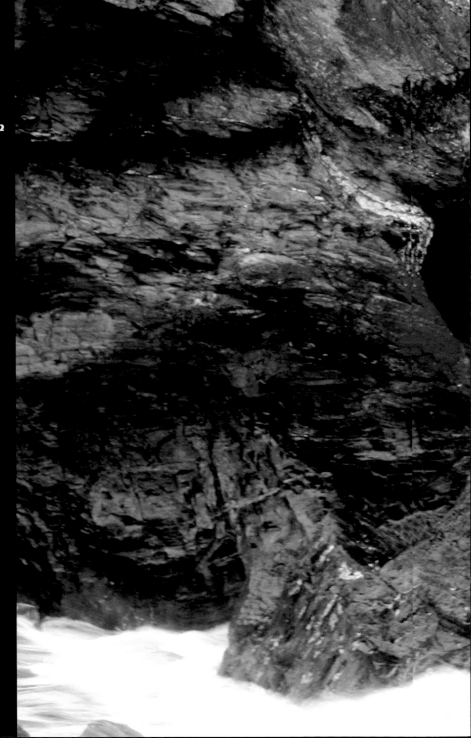

Magic Caves

Mysterious entrances to the Underworld realm, caves have always been places of magic and mystery.

Carved into the living rock of Mother Earth to enter a cave is to enter a dark silent world of ancient mystery unaffected by the world outside.

Often seen as the abode of hobgoblins and faeries, caves were avoided by superstitious folk.

21. **Merlin's Cave, Cornwall**
    The baby Arthur was hidden here by the wizard Merlin

22. **The Fairies' Cave, Cumbria**
    A magical entrance to the underground faery realm

23. **Hob Holes, Yorkshire**
    The abode of a hob who could cure the whooping cough

24. **Hobthrush Hall, Yorkshire**
    A forgotten dwelling that was home to a hobgoblin

25. **King Arthur's Cave, Herefordshire**
    King Arthur's treasure is said to lie hidden here under a spell

26. **Alderley Edge, Cheshire**
    The Wizard of Edge and the sleeping knights

27. **Calf Hole, Yorkshire**
    Where the fairies were seen dancing in the pale moonlight

28. **Merlin's Cave, Gwynedd**
    Merlin lies buried here with the thirteen treasures of Britain

29. **St. Fillan's Cave, Fife**
    Home to a mystical saint with a luminous hand

30. **The Fairy Church, Cumbria**
    The fairies here could grant wishes at a nearby well

Merlin's Cave lies beneath Tintagel Castle, the legendary birthplace of King Arthur. An old tale tells how Merlin hid the newborn Arthur in the cave to evade the enemies of the Pendragon crown. Today the cave is flooded by the sea twice a day and can only be accessed at low tide. The ghost of the wizard Merlin is said to haunt the cave.

Previous pages: Waves crashing around Merlin's Cave at high tide. *Inset above:* Starfish in Merlin's Cave. *Above:* Merlin's Cave after the waves recede. *Opposite main:* Tintagel Haven at low tide. *Opposite inset:* Steps leading down to Tintagel Head and King Arthur's castle.

22 The Fairies' Cave

Whitbarrow Scar, Cumbria

A secret cave hidden at the end of a small wooded gully which leads into a Magical Underworld realm.

Main picture: Magical white flowstone formations in the fairies' cave. *Inset below:* The gully leading to the fairies' cave. *Inset above:* A natural fairy wishing well inside the Fairies' Cave.

23. hob holes

Hob Holes near Runswick Bay was once the home of a helpful little spirit known as a Hob. Here was a small cave where local people would take their children to the hob to cure them of the whooping cough (known locally as the kink cough).

The following rhyme had to be recited to the hob in order to effect a cure:

"Hob Hole Hob,
My bairn's gotten t'kink cough,
Tak it off,
Tak it off."

Left: Inside one of the Hob Holes in Runswick Bay. *Above*: The Hob Holes.

24. hobthrush hall

over silton, north yorkshire

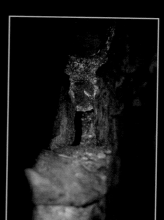

Main: The interior of Hobthrush Hall cave.
Above: One of the many large shiny spiders
that now inhabit the cave. *Right*: A tiny
secret doorway in Hobthrush Hall, only a
couple of inches high!

Located in the scars (cliffs) on the edge of
the North York Moors this lonely cave is
now all but forgotten.

In past times it was better known as the
abode of a local hobgoblin who could perform
great athletic feats such as jumping to the
nearby Carlow Hill in a single stride.

This friendly hob would help the local
innkeeper by churning his cream at night in
return for a slice of bread and butter.

Deep within the spider-infested cave you
may find a tiny doorway where perhaps the
hob still hides from unwelcome guests.

25. King Arthur's Cave

Little Doward, Herefordshire

King Arthur buried his treasure here when he was on the run from his enemies. Merlin then cast a spell over the cave to ensure that the treasure could never be found.

King Vortigern's huge hillfort sits opposite the cave.

Main: King Arthur's Cave

26. Alderley Edge

Alderley Edge, Cheshire

Long ago a farmer was crossing the Edge in order to sell his beautiful white mare at the market. Upon reaching the Thieves' Hole the horse stopped and refused to move forward, for out of nowhere appeared an old man dressed in a dark flowing gown with long hair and a beard. The old man offered to buy the horse but the farmer rudely refused believing he would receive a better price at the market.

To the farmer's surprise and disappointment the horse was admired by all at the market but nobody was willing to buy. Leaving the market behind him the farmer once again crossed over the Edge in low spirits and cursing his luck. When the farmer reached the Thieves' Hole he was amazed to see the old man waiting for him. He bade the farmer to follow and led him to a large rock embedded in the hillside.

The old man touched the rock with his staff and with a sound like thunder the rock split in two and revealed a pair of Iron Gates. With this the horse reared and the farmer fell to his knees begging for mercy. The old wizard told the farmer not to be afraid and led both man and beast along a passage and into a large cavern full of sleeping knights. Beside all but one knight was a white mare which was also in enchanted sleep. The wizard led the farmer into another cavern full of jewels and bade him to take his fill as payment for the horse. The farmer grabbed what he could and left hastily the way he had come.

The farmer returned on many occasions to search for the Iron Gates but his efforts were in vain. From that day to this people have scoured the Edge trying to locate the Gates but none have ever found them.

Main: An entrance to one of the many endless mines and caverns on Alderney Edge. *Above left*: A pub sign showing the wizard from the tale. *Above middle*: The Wishing Well on Alderney Edge with adjoining hermit's cave. *Above right*: Carving of the wizard's head by the Wizard's Well. The inscription says *"Drink of this and take thy fill for the water falls by the Wizard's Will"*.

27. Calf Hole

Skirethorns, North Yorkshire

"In olden days a dwelling of Fairies; inside have been found small and curious pipes, called by the natives 'fairy pipes.' Aged people still tell how, in their youth, the fairies were often seen dancing in the bright moonlight."

Main: View from inside Calf Hole. *Inset*: Calf Hole exterior.

28. Merlin's Cave

Bardsey Island, Gwynedd

Bardsey Island lies off the tip of the Llyn Peninsular in North Wales. It was once an important place of pilgrimage and it is said that 20,000 saints lie buried there.

One side of the island rises sharply and it is on this hillside that a tiny cave known as Merlin's Cave can be found. Merlin the wizard is said to have been imprisoned on this island in a castle of glass with the thirteen treasures of Britain. Could this be the cave where Merlin lay hidden in slumber?

By a farm at the base of the hill a unique apple tree grows. This rare and ancient breed of apple is known as Merlin's apple. Perhaps this story relates to the legendary Island of Avalon from Arthurian legend "The Isle of Apples"?

Main: Bardsey Island, known as Ynys Enlli in Welsh contains a ruined monastery and was a place of pilgrimage in ancient times. *Below*: The entrance to the tiny Merlin's Cave lies between three white quartz boulders on the hillside. You'll have to crawl on your belly to get inside to the little hermit's cell.

29. St. Fillan's Cave

Pittenweem, Fife

St. Fillan was said to have lived as a hermit in this cave in the 7th century. There was no light inside the cave so he read by the light of a ghostly glow that emanated from his hand.

In later years people were left in this cave overnight as a cure for lunacy. A secret passage leads to the Abbey above while a natural holy well in the cave has curative powers.

The cave has been used in the past for smuggling and storage but nowadays has been consecrated as a chapel to St. Fillan.

Main: The far reaches of the cave where the holy well can be found. *Left inset*: The entrance to St. Fillan's Cave on Cove Wynd. *Right inset:* The holy well formed by water dripping from natural flowstone formations.

Main: The chapel and altar. *Inset left:* The 'secret' passageway to the abbey. *Inset right*: The entranceway to St. Fillan's Cave with a painting of the saint.

30. Fairy Church

Humphrey Head, Cumbria

This natural rock arch known as the Fairy Church is situated on a remote headland. Beneath it lay a well where local people would make offerings of bent pins to the fairies in exchange for wishes. Nearby is another holy well that has curative powers.

Left: The Fairy Church viewed from above. *Top*: Humphrey Head. *Bottom*: The Fairy Church viewed from the sands below.

Directions to Magic Caves

21. Merlin's Cave
Tintagel, Cornwall
Follow the trail down from the village of Tintagel towards Tintagel castle until you come to a sandy bay. Merlin's Cave is the first cave on the left side - SX050890 (unmarked)

22. The Fairies' Cave
Witherslack Hall, Cumbria
Follow the lane North from Witherslack Hall for about 1km. Take the footpath on your right heading Northeast. Follow the footpath through the woods to the foot of Whitbarrow Scar, then follow the edge of the hill northwards until you see the gully leading to the fairies' cave on your right - SD433877 (seek permission first)

23. Hob Holes
Runswick Bay, North Yorkshire
Park by the shore in Runswick Bay and walk South along the beach until you see the caves to your right - NZ814155

24. Hobthrush Hall
Over Silton, North Yorkshire
Follow the footpath West out of the village of Over Silton and then turn North following the base of the wooded cliffs until you spot the cave high up on your right - SE449936 (unmarked)

25. King Arthur's Cave
Little Doward, Herefordshire
Follow the lane running Southeast past Doward Farm. Just before you reach the U bend at the very bottom of the lane look out for a stile on your right. Cross the stile and follow the public footpath along the edge of the wood to the cave. - SO545155

26. Alderley Edge
Alderley Edge, Cheshire
Take the public footpath Eastwards from the town of Alderley Edge and walk along the path near the top edge of the wooded escarpment until you pass the Wizard's Well - SJ854780 and the Wishing Well - SJ858778. Entrances to the mines can be found all along the Edge. The Thieves Hole is in the small wood at SJ861772

27. Calf Hole
Skirethorns, North Yorkshire
From the Northern end of Threshfield village take Skirethorns Lane Westwards towards Skirethorns. When you reach the T junction at the end turn right down Wood Lane and continue for just over a mile until you see the cave in the scar (cliffs) behind you to your left - SD963646 (seek permission first)

28. Bardsey Island
Aberdaron, Gwynedd
From Aberdaron travel south to Porth Meudwy to catch a boat to Bardsey Island. Advance booking is required. To find Merlin's Cave look out for the three white quartz boulders forming a triangle on the hillside. Take the path opposite Plas Bach where the sacred apple tree grows - SH121219 (unmarked)

29. St. Fillan's Cave
Pittenweem, Fife
The entrance to the cave is on Cove Wynd in the village of Pittenweem. The gate is locked so you have to collect the key from The Cocoa Tree Shop & Cafe on the High Street - NO550025

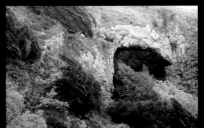

30. The Fairy Church
Allithwaite, Cumbria
From Allithwaite take the lane leading South to Humphrey Head. Once you reach the gate at the end of the lane that leads onto the sands, park and look for a trackway near the gate that leads up the side of the headland. Continue South along the headland until you see that Fairy Church below on your right. - SD390738

Sacred Springs

In Pagan times the landscape of Britain was littered with Sacred Springs which our ancestors revered for their magical healing properties and as portals to the mysterious underworld of spirits.

The early church adopted these sacred places and renamed them as Holy Wells, attributing their healing properties to local saints.

After the reformation the Church tried to put an end to all such reverence and many old traditions were outlawed, abandoned and forgotten.

Yet in a few small hidden places the traditions and folklore persisted and still continue to this present day. In a handful of mystical locations the healing waters can still perform their ancient magic.

Sacred Springs

31. Chalice Well

Glastonbury, Somerset

The magical waters of the Chalice Well flow directly from the mysterious underworld beneath Glastonbury Tor. Pilgrims have been visiting this place for centuries to partake of its healing waters and to visit the spot which legend says Joseph of Arimathea hid the Holy Grail.

The Chalice Well Gardens now surround this magical spring creating a space of quiet retreat and contemplation. The high iron content of the water leaves a red residue wherever it passes, giving this well the alternative name of the Red Spring.

Previous pages: The Chalice Well with iron cover depicting the vesica pisces which symbolises that this place is a crossover point between our world and the Otherworld. *Right*: The outflow from the Chalice Well cascades over a series of falls. The red deposits from the iron rich water give this place the alternative name of the red spring. *Above*: A friendly robin in the Chalice Well gardens.

Inset: An old tankard that was once used for taking the waters of Our Lady's Well. *Main*: The spring where a local man hid from Pam the Fiddler and a host of imps.

32. Our Lady's Well

Threshfield, North Yorkshire

In past times this well was used as a cure for sore eyes. The waters here were also said to provide sanctuary from evil spirits as attested to by a local man who hid in these waters all night after being chased by the ghost of Pam the Fiddler and a host of imps.

33. Sancreed Well

Sancreed, Cornwall

Nowhere else in England are the ancient traditions associated with holy wells kept alive more than in Cornwall. Wells are decorated with ribbons and offerings and the healing waters are resorted to for cures and wishes.

Sat beside the ruins of an ancient chapel Sancreed Well is revered as a place of healing and visions.

The alternative name of the Crone Well could link this place to the ancient Celtic crone goddess.

Left and above: Sancreed Well lies hidden among the trees and undergrowth. Radiation levels in this well have been recorded at over 200 percent above normal. Could this explain some of the strange phenomena that have been reported here? *Right*: Offerings suspended over the entrance to the well.

34. Madron Well & Boswarthen Chapel

Madron, Cornwall

One of Cornwall's most famous healing wells combines pagan cures with Christian blessings. The original Pagan well is hidden away in marshy ground whilst the ruined Christian chapel provides its own magical space in which to soak up the otherworldly atmosphere. Many cures have been recorded here as well as a tradition of offering straw crosses which were placed in the water to float downstream.

Facing page: The interior of Boswarthen chapel with a small enclosure in the corner which houses the Christian well. *Left*: The natural pagan well is overhung by a tree covered with offerings. *Top & middle*: Handmade offerings left near the pagan well. *Bottom*: Water flowing into the well chamber of Boswarthen chapel.

St. Winefride's Well has been effecting miraculous cures for centuries. Dozens of ancient crutches can be found here left by those who were crippled before they came here to partake of the healing waters.

Legend says that the well was formed in the 7th century on the spot where St. Winefride's head landed when it was cut off by her attacker.

"And on the spot where her blood had flowed there was an earthquake, with a loud noise, and a great stream of water burst forth, and has continued to flow from that day to this."

Her head was restored to her body by St. Bueno with only a thin scar visible around her neck. She was then told to sit on a magical stone in the well to pray and so was healed.

Nowadays people still come to the well to be cured, bathing three times in the waters and sitting upon St. Bueno's Stone.

Left: The chamber where the sacred spring emerges. *Above*: St. Winefride's Chapel. *Right*: The pool where pilgrims bathe and sit upon St. Bueno's Stone to be healed.

36. Tecla's Well

Llandegla, Denbighshire

This magical spring is able to cure epilepsy. The sufferer must bathe in the well at dusk, leave an offering, and then walk three times around the church carrying a chicken under their arm. They must then sleep under the communion table and if the chicken is dead by the morning then the epilepsy will be cured!

Main: Tecla's Well with stone offering cup. *Inset:* Sign by the well showing how to effect a cure using a chicken.

37. Well of Age

Isle of Iona, Argyll and Bute

Tobar nah Aois, the Well of Age, is a fabled fountain of youth. If you bathe your face in it's waters three times at sunrise you will roll back the years and appear youthful and

38. Old Man's Mouth & The Giant Wade

East Ayton, North Yorkshire.

The Old Man is a legendary local giant known as Wade. He constructed the nearby Wade's Causeway and his grave is marked by a standing stone known as Wade's Stone.

Inset top: Wade's Causeway, a mysterious ancient trackway running across the North York Moors. *Inset left:* Wade's stone is said to mark the burial place of the legendary giant. Strange phenomena have been reported by those standing near it. *Main:* The Old Man's Mouth.

39. The Ebbing & Flowing Well

Giggleswick, North Yorkshire

This magical well has a curious property which causes the water level to rise and fall as you watch.

Legend tells how a nymph was chased here by a horned satyr who was overcome with lust for her. The nymph prayed to the gods and was saved by being turned into a fountain of water emerging from the earth. This well became famous as a place of healing, but the only sign remaining of the nymph is her breath which causes the well water to ebb and flow like the tides.

Left: The Ebbing and Flowing Well sits in a stone enclosure beneath the wooded hillside of Giggleswick Scar. *Above:* Sit by the side of the Ebbing and Flowing Well for a while and you will see the water level miraculously rise and fall like the slow inward and outward breath of the water nymph.

40. Lady Keld Spring

CROPTON, NORTH YORKSHIRE

The Lady Keld Spring at the high end of Cropton village was once the home of a company of evil water elves. These spirits were eventually driven away by three witches who conducted 'a most heathen ceremony' at the site.

Main picture: St. Gregory's church, Cropton. A path leads from here past an old motte into woodland which contains the Lady Keld Spring. *Inset left*: The well in Cropton village which is 300ft deep and said to contain the finest water in the district. *Inset right:* The Lady Keld Spring is hidden in the woodland North of Cropton and feeds into Cropton Beck.

Directions to the Sacred Springs

31. The Chalice Well
Glastonbury, Somerset
The Chalice Well Gardens are located on the corner of Chilkwell Street and Wellhouse Lane, just Southeast of Glastonbury town centre - ST506385 (entrance fee payable)

32. Threshfield Lady's Well
Grassington, North Yorkshire
Head West out of Grassington and cross the River Wharfe at Grassington bridge. Immediately after the bridge take the road to the left. After less than 100m there is a small gap in the wall to the left. Pass through the gap and follow the short path down to the well - SD997637 (unmarked and in a private garden)

33. Sancreed Well
Sancreed, Cornwall
Take the public footpath opposite Sancreed church, heading West. Keep to the right and you will reach the well after about 300m - SW417292

34. Madron Well
Madron, Cornwall
Take the B3312 Fore Street West from Madron. After about 500m turn right down a track. After another 300m take the right fork down a public footpath. The original pagan well is hidden away in the marshy ground to your left when you reach the tree covered in rags. The Christian well and chapel are further on - SW445327

35. St. Winefride's Well
Holywell, Flintshire
On the B5121 New Road, just North of the town centre - SJ185762 (small entrance fee payable).

36. Tecla's Well
Llandegla, Denbighshire
Take the public footpath heading South out of Llandegla. After about 100m the well is on the right near the river - SJ194522.

37. The Well of Age
Iona, Argyll and Bute
From the jetty take the road North until you see a path on the left heading to the summit of the highest hill which is called Dun I. Once you reach the summit search the Northern edge until you find the pool - NM284253 (unmarked)

38. The Ebbing & Flowing Well
Giggleswick, North Yorkshire
The Ebbing and Flowing Well is located right by the side of the B6480 about 1500m North of Giggleswick - SD803653 (look out for traffic)

39. Old Man's Mouth
East Ayton, North Yorkshire
Old Man's Mouth is located on the East side of the road which runs through Forge Valley north of East Ayton - SE984871 (unmarked). Wade's Causeway is located on Wheeldale Moor south of Egton Bridge - SE804973. Wade's Stone can be found in a field just Southwest of Goldsborough - NZ830143

40. Lady Keld, Cropton
Cropton, North Yorkshire
Follow the public footpath that passes down the right hand side of St. Gregory's Church in Cropton. This leads downhill through woodland for about 500m before emerging into a grassy field. The Lady Keld Springs lie in a wooded gully on the far side of the field - SE755899 (fence blocks path, seek permission first)

Fairy Wells

At a handful of locations in Britain the ancient Pagan customs have persisted despite centuries of repression. Simple country folk would still at times seek the help of the fairies to fulfil their wishes.

Bent pins, coins and other small offerings would be left at these wells in the hope of receiving some small help from the Fair Folk.

Some of these natural springs became known simply as Wishing Wells, while others still carry tales of Faery magic from times gone by.

Fairy Wishing Wells

41. Harmby Fairy Well

Harmby, North Yorkshire

The Fairy Well in Harmby emerges in a field under a pair of Hawthorn Trees. Look out for fairy lights in the twilight here!

Previous pages: A spring of fresh water gushes forth from the Fairy Well in a field just outside the village of Harmby. *Above*: Blossoming hawthorns stand over the fairy well. Hawthorns are known as 'fairy trees' in the Celtic lands.

42. Diana's Well

East Witton, North Yorkshire

A survival of Roman paganism, the water from Diana's well emerges from a carved stone head while inside is a grotto with a stone table and a basin of pure clean well water. In past times visitors would cast pins into this well to make wishes. A local rhyme states:

'Whoever eats Hammer Nuts
and drinks Diana's water
Will never leave Witton Town
while he's a rag or tatter.'

Left: Water emerges from the carved stone head outside of Diana's Well. *Top*: The wellhouse chamber with stone table. *Bottom*: A stone basin of crystal clear water inside the wellhouse.

43. St. Anne's Well

Trellech, Monmouthshire

The fairies used to dance around this well on Midsummer's Eve and All Hallow's Eve. They would drink from harebell cups which local people would find scattered around the next morning and take home for use in magical cures.

A local man was unable to draw water from the well after digging up a fairy ring. One day he met a small wizened old man by the well who told him to replace the turfs. He did so and then was able to draw the water again!

This well has been used both for cures and for wishes. Drop a small stone into the well and count the bubbles to see how many months it will take for your wish to come true. It's healing properties have given it the alternative name of the Virtuous Well.

Frogs and newts live in this well, so take care not to disturb them! It is also visited often by local wildlife, so keep silent and be still and who knows what you may experience in this magical place!

Opposite main: A magical frog sitting beside St. Anne's Well. *Opposite inset:* A frog floating in the well water. *Main:* St. Anne's Well sits inside a stone enclosure while above it people have hung rags to the trees to make wishes. *Inset left:* A newt found inside the well. *Inset below:* The tiny enclosure that houses the wellhead is strewn with offerings to the fairies.

44. Carreg Cennan

Llandeilo, Carmarthenshire

Hidden beneath this spectacular Medieval castle lies a long dark tunnel leading to a tiny fairy wishing well.

Bent pins were placed in this well in order to make wishes and can still be found in the well to this day.

Main: The fairy wishing well under Carreg Cennen Castle. *Right*: Part of the underground passage leading to the wishing well. *Below*: Carreg Cennan Castle hides the secret wishing well.

45. Tam Lin's Well

Selkirk, Scottish Borders

Main: Tamlane's Well flows out into a stone trough by the side of the road. The red colour comes from the iron content of the water. *Below:* The original well is hidden in the woods behind (ask permission first).

Tam Lin was abducted by the Queen of the Fairies and held captive in the woods around Caterhaugh. One day a young woman met him there and became pregnant with his baby. In order to rescue her lover from the Fairies she was instructed to grab hold of him as he rode by with them on Hallowe'en. When she did so he changed into all kinds of beastly shapes as she gripped onto him and eventually when he turned into a burning coal she cast him into the well. He then changed back to human form and was freed from his Fairy enchantment. The well subsequently became known as Tam Lin's Well (Tamlane's Well)

TAMLANE'S WELL

46. St. Blane's Fairy Well

Kingarth, Isle of Bute

The ruins of St. Blane's Church lie on the site of an ancient monastery, one of the first of it's kind in the British Isles. The walls of the monastery and the foundations of some of the ancient monks' cells still exist in this secluded wooded location near the southern tip of the Isle of Bute.

The site contains a healing Fairy Well and a strange circular enclosure called the Devil's Cauldron. Folklore tells that within the Devil's Cauldron there once grew a pine tree that had the magical property to bestow prophetic visions upon those who left a sprig of its leaves under their pillow at night.

Main: The ruined remains of St. Blane's Church.
Right: The Fairy Well is now covered by an iron grille.

47. St. Queran's Well

Cargen, Dumfries and Galloway

This well, dedicated to a 9th century saint was once a fairy wishing well as attested to by the large number of coins and bent pins that were found when the well was later excavated.

Main: St. Queran's Well with clootie rags attached to a nearby tree as offerings. *Inset:* A recent addition to the well, the iron face of St. Queran.

48. Uny's Wishing Well

Carbis Bay, Cornwall

Secreted away in the wooded cliffs above St. Ives Bay is this magical little wishing well. In times gone by folk would leave bent pins and other offerings to the fairies in return for healing and wishes.

A regular flow of clear fresh water fills a stone cut basin before cascading away over the cliff edge to the sands far below.

Left: The wishing well is overhung with offerings left to the fairies. *Top*: The cliffs that hide the spring. *Bottom*: The outflow from the spring tumbles down the cliff face.

Directions to the Fairy Wells

41. The Fairy Well
Harmby, North Yorkshire
Follow the public footpath that leads West out of Harmby for about 400m. The Fairy Well lies just to the south of the footpath - SE124896

42. Diana's Well
East Witton, North Yorkshire
Head South out of East Witton down Sowden Beck Road. until you come to the woods on Witton Fell. Take the second trackway to the right into the woods and follow it for about 700m. Diana's Well is on the left - SE136850 (marked as Cast-away Well, seek permission first)

43. St. Anne's Well
Trellech, Monmouthshire
Head South out of Trellech and take the right fork in the road. St. Anne's Well is on the left after about 200m - SO503051

44. Carreg Cennan
Llandeilo, Carmarthenshire
Head South from Llandeilo to Trap and follow the signs for Carreg Cennen Castle. Entrance fee is payable at the castle which includes access to the tunnel. Tunnel entrance can be found at the far corner of the castle courtyard - SN667191 (bring a torch)

45. Tam Lin's Well
Selkirk, Scottish Borders
Take the B7009 Southwest out of Selkirk. After about 5km turn right onto the B7039. Tam Lin's Well is on the left after about 800m right next to the road - NT437268

46. St. Blane's Fairy Well
Kingarth, Argyll and Bute
Take the A844 West out of Kingarth and then the first left down Plan Lane. Drive about 3km to the very end of Plan Lane and park. Then walk down the trackway on the left heading Northeast to St. Blane's Church - NS094534

47. St. Queran's Well
Cargen, Dumfries and Galloway
Take the A170 South out of Dumfries and when you reach the 90 degree left turn in the road at Islesteps continue straight on down the track instead. Continue for about 1km until you reach a stream called Crooks Pow. The well is just to the right before you cross the stream - NX956722

48. Uny's Wishing Well
Carbis Bay, Cornwall
Follow the clifftop path East out of Carbis Bay. Just before you reach the top of the highest cliff there is a small, easily missed track to your left which forks off through the trees and down the face of the cliff to the well - SW535384

Mystic Mountains

Mountains have always been places of retreat and contemplation. Touching the sky lonely mountaintops have been sought out since ancient times by those wishing to contemplate the heavens above and the world below.

Bards would climb to the tops of mountains to seek inspiration for their poetic compositions and music. Spending several nights up there would enable them to experience intense visions.

Mountains are also the retreats of spirits and the ghosts of ancient warriors. Many mountains have legends of sleeping knights who lie under their summits waiting for the day when they will be called upon again.

Lonely, windswept and haunted places, mountains can seem like a world apart from the more settled lands below.

51. Blencathra, Cumbria
Sleeping knights lie in waiting under this summit

52. Glastonbury Tor, Somerset
Entrance to the underworld and a place of intense magic and mystery

53. Cadbury Castle, Somerset
The ancient site of Camelot where King Arthur leads the wild hunt

54. Cadair Idris, Gwynedd
Spend a night on the summit and you will go insane or become a poet

55. Dinas Emrys, Gwynedd
The boy Merlin escaped sacrifice here by discovering dragons below

56. Holyhead Mountain, Anglesey
A holy mountain on a holy island

57. Sewingshields Crags, Northumberland
A local farmer follows his ball of wool into an underground realm

58. Hood Hill, Yorkshire
A place of druid sacrifice

59. Schiehallion, Perthshire
The Fairy Hill of the Caledonians

Mystic Mountains

51. BLENCATHRA

Threlkeld, Cumbria

Curious legends relate to several hills in the **B**ritish **I**sles, under which are said to lie a company of sleeping warriors waiting for the day when they will be needed again to save the island of **B**ritain from invaders. **T**ales relate how hapless travellers have stumbled upon these hidden caverns heaped with gold and have caused the angry knights to awaken early from their slumber.

Blencathra means "**D**evil's **P**eak" and it is said that an army of warriors lies sleeping below its summit awaiting the call to arms.

Previous pages: The summit of Blencathra under a dark moody sky.
This page: View from the eminence of Blencathra over the settled lands below.

52. Glastonbury Tor

Glastonbury, Somerset

Glastonbury Tor is a place of intense magic and mystery. The Tor is said to be hollow and contains a mysterious Underworld riddled with hidden caverns. Dragon lines from across the land converge here creating powerful energies. In the past the Somerset marshes surrounding the Tor made it into an island, the fabled "Isle of Avalon".

Above: Looking across the former marshes of the Somerset levels towards Glastonbury Tor, the Isle of Avalon. St. Michael's Tower sits atop the Tor outlined by the sunset.

53. Cadbury Castle

South Cadbury, Somerset

In legend Cadbury Castle is the site of Camelot, and one of the hills under which Arthur and his knights are said to sleep awaiting the time when they will fight for the nation once again. The entrance to their cave is guarded by a giant Iron Gate which opens once every seven years on Midsummer's eve to let Arthur and his warriors ride out into the night. Here we may see an older tradition of the phantom wild hunt mingling with the legend of Arthur, and indeed Arthur is said to lead the wild hunt along a track here known as Arthur's Hunting Path.

If you wash your face in Arthur's Well on Midsummer's Eve your dreams will show you the entrance to Arthur's Cave and the sleeping warriors inside the hill.

Another story tells of an enormous winged dragon that flew nightly over the Exe Valley, lighting up the sky with its flaming breath. He flew back and forth between Dolbury Hill and Cadbury Castle guarding two hordes of treasure. A local saying goes...

"If Cadbury Castle and Dolbury Hill delven were
All England might plough with a golden share"

Right: View from the ramparts of the Iron Age hillfort of Cadbury Castle. *Left*: King Arthur's Well, a natural spring near the summit of Cadbury Castle.

54. CADAIR IDRIS

Dolgellau, Gwynedd

On the summit of Cadair Idris is a stone bed, the Bed of Idris. It is said that anyone who spends the night on the summit in Idris's Bed will either become a poet or go insane.

Fairies lived on Cadair Idris and would descend from the mountain in disguise to visit the local people. They rewarded good hospitality and a particularly genial man called Morgan Rhys was gifted with a fairy harp that would play any tune he wanted by simply touching his fingers to the strings.

This page: The summits of Cadair Idris viewed from the East. *Next page:* Llyn Cau, one of the magical lakes on Cadair Idris lying just below the summit.

The lakes on Cadair Idris are said to be connected by underground caverns. Throw a stick into one of the lakes and it is said it will eventually appear in one of the others.

Anyone who attempts to divert water from these lakes will incur the wrath of the mountain spirits and will be driven away with thunder and lightning.

55. Dinas Emrys

Beddgelert, Gwynedd

The hill of Dinas Emrys, overlooked by the Snowdonia Mountains, is the scene of one of Britain's earliest documented legends.

The 9th century manuscript, Historia Britonum, describes how King Vortigern was attempting to build a fortress here to protect his people from the marauding Saxons, but each time he built a tower it would collapse the next day. A child called Myrddin Emrys was brought here as a sacrifice to appease the spirits of the mountain but instead of being sacrificed the boy, who was actually the young wizard Merlin, advised the King that the foundations of his castle were being disturbed by two dragons in a lake beneath the hill, a red dragon and a white dragon.

Vortigern had his men dig down and drain the lake. The two dragons then fought a terrible battle and the white dragon was driven away by the red. Vortigern was then able to build his fortress and named it Dinas Emrys in honour of the boy Merlin.

This tale is said to signify the defeat of the white dragon of the Saxons by the red dragon of the Welsh.

Previous page: View from the summit of Dinas Emrys. *This page:* Part of the hidden world that lies at the summit of Dinas Emrys.

The summit of Dinas Emrys contains a mystical landscape of overgrown ruins. Remains of fortresses from prehistoric to Medieval times litter the hilltop.

56. holyhead Mountain

holyhead, Isle of Anglesey

Holyhead Island is the most sacred place on Anglesey and contains its highest mountain called Holyhead Mountain. Anglesey was the most sacred island of the Druids and so this place must have held some special significance in times gone by.

A saint known as St. Cybi had his cell here and would meet weekly at Clorach Wells in Llandyfrydog with St. Seiriol, who had himself travelled from Penmon Priory on the opposite side of Anglesey. Because St. Cybi left in the morning heading East, and returned in the evening heading West he always had the sun in his face and so was known as Cybi the Tanned. St. Seriol travelling in the opposite direction and never towards the sun was known as Seiriol the Fair.

Perhaps this tale relates a more ancient mystical connection between these two sacred sites?

Penmon Priory, on the opposite side of Anglesey, was founded by St. Seiriol in the 6th century. Here you will find St. Seiriol's Healing Well still encased in its own ancient stone wellhouse.

Previous page: View from the summit of Holyhead Mountain. *This page:* Penmon Priory.

57. Sewingshields

Haydon Bridge, Northumberland

In the cavernous castle vaults below the site of Sewingshield Castle, still hidden beneath the hills lie King Arthur, Queen Guinevere and his band of warrior knights, sleeping soundly until the British Nation calls on their help. Beside them, on a table, sit a horn, a sheathed sword and a garter. To awaken the great King, it is said one must draw the sword, cut the garter and blow the horn.

A local farmer was once sat amongst the castle ruins knitting, when his ball of wool got away from him and fell down a crack in his rocky resting place. The local man just managed to squeeze through and follow his runaway knitting into the legendary chamber below. Everything was arranged as tradition had insisted. He drew the sword and cut the garter, but re-sheathed his weapon and neglected to blow the horn! Arthur awoke but for a moment, to briefly exclaim:

> "O Woe betide that evil day
> On which this witless wight was born,
> Who drew the sword, the garter cut,
> But never blew the bugle-horn..."

Right: The rocky escarpment of Sewingshields Crags. *Above*: The Emperor Hadrian's Roman Wall runs along the top of Sewingshields Crags.

58. hood hill

kilburn, yorkshire

Hood Hill was a place of druid sacrifice. At the summit of the hill was their altar where they made offerings to their pagan gods. Local legend says that Christian priests chased out these druids along with the devil himself, who left his footprint in one of the rocks on Hood Hill.

The summit of Hood Hill is now a magical, lonely place topped by the remains of an ancient 'fairy' fort.

Main: Hood Hill in late autumn viewed from Sutton Bank. *Above*: Magical trees crowning the summit of Hood Hill in wintertime. *Below*: Steps leading up to the fort on top of Hood Hill.

59. Schiehallion

Braes of Foss, Perthshire

Known as "The Fairy Hill of the Caledonians" the mountain of Schiehallion is regarded as the centre of all Scotland and is home to the hag goddess the Cailleach Beara.

This impressive holy mountain hides a natural spring where maidens made offerings to the fairies on Beltaine (May Day). There is also a magical cave known as Tom-a-mhorair which is an entrance to the Otherworld realm of the Fairies. But be careful if you enter for it is said that it's doors only open one way and you may never get out!

Fairy Queen Mab used to hold court on this mountain and fairy tribes from far and wide would congregate here.

A story is also told of a hunchback who crossed the mountain and was cured by the fairies because they enjoyed his beautiful singing. His tuneless friend was less fortunate however and was cursed by the fairies and turned into a deformed giant with a double hump!

Main: Approaching Schiehallion from the South. *Inset*: Some old shielings near the location of the mysterious cave.

Directions to Mystic Mountains

51. Blencathra
Threlkeld, Cumbria
Park at the Blencathra Centre above the village of Threlkeld and take the footpath that leads up the mountain to the summit - NY322277

52. Glastonbury Tor
Glastonbury, Somerset
Take the A361 (Chilkwell Street) heading East out of Glastonbury town centre. When you get to the Chalice Well Gardens turn left up Wellhouse Lane and then immediately right following the footpath up to the summit of the Tor - ST511386

53. Cadbury Castle
South Cadbury, Somerset
Park in the car park just South of South Cadbury and follow the trail up to the summit. King Arthur's Well is just to the left of the path before you reach the highest rampart - ST627251

54. Cadair Idris
Dolgellau, Gwynedd
Take the A470 East out of Dolgellau, then the A487 Southwest until you reach Minffordd. Take the right fork in the village and park at the campsite. You can then follow the public footpath all the way up to the summit past Llyn Cau - SH711130

55. Dinas Emrys
Beddgelert, Gwynedd
Take the A498 Eastwards out of Beddgelert and after about 1km park at Carflwyn Hall on the left. There is a sign there showing various walks including one to the summit of Dinas Emrys. Pass by Carflwyn Hall and turn right just before the Community Allotment and follow the trail to the summit - SH606492

56. Holyhead Mountain
Holyhead, Isle of Anglesey
Take the road heading Northwest out of Holyhead until you reach the Holyhead Breakwater Country Park. Park there and follow the trail up to the summit. (Parking fee payable). SH218829. Penmon Priory is 45 minutes drive East in the village of Penmon - SH630807

57. Sewingshields
Haydon Bridge, Northumberland
Take the road North out of Haydon Bridge until you reach the B6318 which follows Hadrian's Wall. Turn left then take the first right towards Sewingshields farm. When you reach Hadrian's Wall turn left through the woods and follow the crags for about 1km until you reach the summit - NY800700

58. Hood Hill
Kilburn, North Yorkshire
Follow the lane West out of the village of Kilburn and when you get to the woods park in the car park on the right. Follow the path from the car park up to the summit of Hood Hill - SE503814

59. Schiehallion
Braes of Foss, Perth and Kinross
From the Braes of Foss take the footpath that leads South and then West to the summit of Schiehallion - NN714547. The cave is almost impossible to find and is near some old shielings at NN708534 which can be reached by a very long (12km), rough track from Fortinghall

Fairy Hills

These are the fabled Hollow Hills, entrances to the Otherworld realm of the Fairy Folk.

The fairies who reigned in this land long ago were defeated by the iron-wielding invaders. Unable to resist their weapons the fairies retreated to lonely hilltops and eventually were driven underground.

There they passed from being creatures of flesh and blood into mysterious beings with magical powers, seen only occasionally in the twilight and on special nights of the year.

Now no longer seen the fairies have passed into legend, but in a few special places, the fairy hills that were their last strongholds, their presence may still at times be felt.

61. The Fairy Cross Plain

Fryupdale, Yorkshire

The Fairy Cross Plain was a meeting place of the fairies in times gone by and their fairy rings could often be seen in the grass around this area after a night of fairy revelry.

Where the two dales of Little Fryupdale and Great Fryupdale join there is a conspicuous hill called Round Hill which is also known as a Fairy hill.

Many Fairy pathways cross here leading up onto the high ridges all around.

Previous pages: The Fairy Cross Plain viewed from Danby Rigg. *Above*: Round Hill sits at the confluence of Little Fryupdale and Great Fryupdale, near the head of the two dales. *Right*: The fairy hill in winter.

62. Craig y Ddinas

Vale of Neath, Powys

Craig y Ddinas was known as the "Last stronghold of the fairies in Wales". In past times fairies were seen dancing here and tumbling down the hillside in the moonlight.

"Especially does a certain steep and rugged crag there, called Craig y Ddinas, bear a distinctly awful reputation as a stronghold of the fairy tribe. Its caves and crevices have been their favourite haunt for many centuries, and upon this rock was held the court of the last fairies who have ever appeared in Wales."

The hill is also said to contain a chamber full of treasure that is encircled by sleeping warriors. In order to take the treasure one must pass by a bell in a narrow passageway. But take care not to ring the bell or the knights will awaken and beat you black and blue!

Main: View from the summit of Craig y Ddinas

63. Castell Dinas Bran & Gwyn ap Nudd

Llangollen, Denbighshire

St. Collen once climbed this hill to confront the fairy king Gwyn ap Nudd. He entered a secret door in the side of the hill and was led along tunnels, finally emerging into the grand throne room, which was filled with Gwyn's courtiers. Gwyn welcomed Collen warmly and invited him to eat at the feast that had been prepared in his honour, but Collen refused all the fine food and drink that was offered him and instead threw holy water over Gwyn and his court. The vision immediately disappeared and Collen was left standing alone on the hilltop.

Previous page: The fairy hill of Castell Dinas Bran. *This page*: The old castle ruins on the summit of Castell Dinas Bran. A most magical location!

64. Doon Hill & the Rev. Robert Kirk

Aberfoyle, Stirling

Doon Hill is Britain's most famous Fairy Hill. It was here in the 17th century that the Reverend Robert Kirk wrote a manuscript called "The Secret Commonwealth of Elves, Fauns and Fairies".

Robert Kirk was a seventh son and was gifted with the second sight. He used to regularly walk up from his church in Aberfoyle to Doon Hill where he observed the Fairy Folk who lived there.

The Fairies were not pleased with him for writing down their secrets though and so one day they abducted him. People thought that the reverend was dead, but he later appeared in a vision to one of his relatives and told him that he would appear again at his son's baptism, and when he did so his cousin should throw a knife over his head to free him from the Fairies (it is well known that fairies are afraid of iron).

But when the day came his cousin was so shocked to see the apparition of his dead relative that he forgot to throw the knife! So the reverend remained a captive and abides still with the Fairies in their Otherworld realm. Some say that his spirit is trapped within the large pine tree that sits atop Doon Hill.

This page: The wooded slopes of Doon Hill, just outside Aberfoyle. *Opposite*: Footpath leading through the magical woodland to the summit of Doon Hill. *Inset left*: Sign marking the start of the Doon Hill Fairy Trail. *Inset right:* Fairy statue left by a visitor.

Doon Hill Fairy Trail
½ mile Circular Walk

This page: An entrance to the Faery Realm? The tree where the spirit of Robert Kirk is said to reside. *Next page:* The clearing on the summit of Doon Hill contains many trees covered with offerings. *Inset:* Some of the many fairy statues which lie hidden around the glade.

The clearing on the summit of Doon Hill is adorned with offerings, wind chimes and wee fairy statues giving it a magical atmosphere.

It is here that the spirit of the Reverend Robert Kirk still resides. Doon Hill is said to be hollow with many caves inside where the Fairy Folk hide.

Come here, make a wish, and take a magical journey into the realm of the Fae.

65. The Eildon Hills & Thomas the Rhymer

Melrose, Scottish Borders

It was while resting under a tree near the Eildon Hills that Thomas of Ercildoune first met the Fairy Queen dressed in green silk and riding on a grey horse. In exchange for a kiss he had to serve as her consort for seven years in Elfland. They rode off into the Eildon Hills and disappeared into underground caverns that led to the Faery Realm.

Everyone thought that Thomas had died and were amazed when one day he suddenly returned, endowed with the gifts of poetry, prophesy and a tongue that could never lie. Henceforth he was known as Thomas the Rhymer or True Thomas and his prophesies became famous throughout the land.

In the Eildon Hills you may also find a strange mound known as the Lucken Hare where a horse trader called Canobie Dick was led into underground caverns and disturbed a host of ghostly knights.

Main and opposite: The Eildon Hills covered with blossoming heather on a late summer's day. It was here that Thomas of Ercildoune met the fairy queen riding a grey horse.

More Fairy hills...

66. Strathaven fairy mound, Lanarkshire

Hidden down by the Avon Water locals still walk three times around this fairy mound to make a wish from the fairies.

67. Pickwinna's Mound, Worlebury Hill, Weston-Super-Mare

Stones were left by fishermen on Pickwinna's Mound as good luck offerings before going out to sea. Fairies have often been sighted on Worlebury Hill and small dew ponds here are called fairy wells.

68. Sithean Mor, Iona

Sithean Mor (the large fairy mound) sits opposite Sithean Beg (the small fairy mound). People in the past believed that the fairies lived here and could grant wishes. Fairy music was often heard coming from the mound and one day a fisherman with his catch was enticed inside by a fairy maiden. He didn't return for a whole year but when he did his fish was still fresh! He had spent the whole year dancing for the fairies while his friend sat by the mound and begged the fairies to free him.

This is also the place where long ago St. Columba was seen meeting with a host of shining angelic beings. One of his acolytes was spying on him and related the tale but was punished by St. Columba for his disobedience.

69. Willy Howe, East Yorkshire

A man riding past Willy Howe heard sounds of merriment coming from inside. He crept up to have a look and through an open door saw the fairies having a banquet. One of the fairies spotted him and offered him a drink, but knowing that if he drank from the cup he would be trapped forever in Fairyland he instead poured out the contents of the cup and fled with it. The fairies gave chase but could not pursue him across a running stream known as the Gypsey Race. The cup was made of a strange material and was later presented to the King of England.

Run nine times around the mound and place your ear against it and it is said that you will still be able to hear the fairies feasting inside.

Directions to the Fairy Hills

61. Fairy Cross Plain
Danby, North Yorkshire
Take the road South from Danby by Danby Castle into Little Fryupdale. Turn left at the crossroads at the end of the dale and continue for about 1km until you reach Fairy Cross Plain Cottage on the left. Opposite the cottage is a bridleway which leads past the round fairy hill up to Danby Rigg - NZ715048

62. Craig y Ddinas
Pontneddfechan, Powys, Wales
Take the lane East out of Pontneddfechan and park in the car park at the end, just after you cross the bridge. You are now at the foot of Craig y Ddinas. Take the footpath to the summit - SN914080

63. Castell Dinas Bran
Llangollen, Denbighshire, Wales
Take the public footpath that leads up from the town of Llangollen or, for an easier climb, park in the lane behind Castell Dinas Bran to the North and take the shorter path to the summit - SJ223430

64. Doon Hill
Aberfoyle, Stirling
Take Manse Road South out of Aberfoyle, across the bridge, past Kirkton and the cemetery, until you reach a lane on the left. Follow the lane until you reach the sign for the Doon Hill Fairy Trail, then follow the trail up to the summit of Doon Hill - NN525001

65. Eildon Hills
Melrose, Scottish Borders
From Melrose Abbey follow St. Cuthbert's Way, the public footpath that leads South out of Melrose into the Eildon Hills - NT550323

66. Strathaven Fairy Mound
Strathaven, Lanarkshire
Take Newton Road south out of Strathaven. When the road turns sharply left (heading East), continue straight on instead, across the fields until you reach the Avon Water (you will have to step over several fences to do this). The fairy mound is in a clearing by the most southerly bend in the river - NS706428 (unmarked)

67. Pickwinna's Mound
Weston-Super-Mare, Somerset
Follow the seafront North to the old derelict pier. Double back right up Upper Kewstoke Road and then double back left up Camp Road opposite St. Joseph's Church. The path up Worlebury Hill is at the end of Camp Road. Pickwinna's Mound is on the summit of Worlebury Hill - ST313624 (unmarked)

68. Sithean Mor
Isle of Iona, Argyll and Bute
Take the ferry from Fionnphort to the jetty on Iona. Then take the road that heads left down the coast. Follow the road as it turns 90 degrees to the right, and continue inland until you reach a farm on the left called Sithean. The fairy mound is just before the farm gate - NM271236 (unmarked)

69. Willy Howe
Wold Newton, East Yorkshire
Take the road East out of Wold Newton then walk for just over 1km and take the first right. At the T junction at the end turn right down a farm lane towards Willy Howe Farm. You will pass by Willy Howe on your left after 100m - TA061723 (seek permission first to walk on the mound)

Magic & Miracles

Legends of Fairies, Dragons, Witches, Hobgoblins, Giants, Wizards and Saints; the Island of Britain abounds with strange tales of magic and miracles.

Some of this magic resides only in old stories and folk memory, yet at some places the magic is still alive and can be felt and experienced to this day.

A trip to one of these places is a journey into the realm of magic and mystery.

Magic & Miracles

71. Merlindale

Drumelzier, Scottish Borders

Merlindale is associated with the legends of Myrddin Wyllt, also known as Merlin of the Woods.

After the death of King Arthur at the battle of Camlann, Merlin retreated here and became a crazed wild man, living like a beast in the forest.

Although some stories say that he later converted to Christianity he died the Druidic triple death of falling, drowning and stabbing. He fell into the River Tweed and was impaled on a sharp branch with his head under the water. His grave lies beside the River Tweed not far from a stone called Merlin's Standing Stone. Merlin's Altar Stone can be found further up the valley.

The lofty ruins of Tinnis Castle sit on an Iron-Age hillfort overlooking the valley and must once have been visited by Merlin.

An unrelated legend from past times tells how the spirit of the River Tweed once made love to the Lord of Drumelzier's wife while he was away on a crusade. The resulting child later went by the name of Tweedie!

Previous pages: Merlindale with Tinnis Castle in the centre. Did the wizard Merlin once stand on this hill? *Left*: View of Merlindale from Tinnis Castle. From here you can see the entire valley of the Tweed with Merlin's Standing Stone in the distance. *Right*: Merlin's standing stone. Nearby is Merlin's Grave.

72 Fairy Steps

Beetham, Cumbria

The **Whin Scar** plateau is a dramatic and magical landscape of limestone pavement and karst formations. The **Fairy Steps** cut through the cliff that borders the plateau, providing access to the mysterious heights above. If you can walk down the fairy steps without touching the sides it is said that you will see the fairies and be granted a wish.

Left: The Fairy Steps lead up through a cut in the edge of the Whin Scar plateau. *Bottom*: A yew tree by the edge of Whin Scar. *Top*: A crack on the edge of Whin Scar forms a cave.

73. Nevern Churchyard

Nevern, Pembrokeshire

The Bleeding Yew tree at Nevern 'bleeds' an unidentifiable red liquid that has baffled scientists. The liquid trickles down the bole and as it does so it congeals and blackens. According to legend, a monk was hung from the tree and it has bled ever since. The man declared his innocence and as he did so proclaimed that: "If you hang me guiltless as I am, the tree will bleed for me". The legend also states that the tree will continue to bleed until a Welshman sits on the throne in Nevern.

Eight old yews, thought to be about 600 years old, intertwine to form a tunnel leading from the church gate to the door of the church. The "bleeding tree" is the second tree on the right.

Opposite: The bleeding yew tree in Nevern churchyard. *Left*: The 10th century Nevern Cross, a rare survival from an earlier age. *Above*: Nevern churchyard.

74. Isle Maree

Loch Maree, Highland

Isle Maree has been a sacred island since ancient times. It is unlike any other island on the loch, being covered with oaks and holly said to have been planted here by the Druids long ago. The Druids also built a stone circle here which can still be seen. Bull sacrifices associated with the Celtic festival of Lughnasa were conducted here until the 17th century.

This tiny island also contained a holy well which was said to cure lunacy. The unfortunate patient had to circle the island three times in a boat, being dunked underwater each time, before drinking from the well.

Next to the well is a money tree where people have made wishes for centuries by hammering coins into the tree. But take care not to remove anything from the island! Bad luck is said to befall any who do so.

This may also be the sacred island where the Celtic crone goddess, the Cailleach, came to drink each spring from the Well of Youth to be transformed into the goddess Bride, the goddess of spring who would turn the earth green again.

This page: Islands on Loch Maree. *Opposite main*: The burial ground lies within the ancient Druid circle. Grave slabs of all ages can be found here, including the one in the foreground which recalls a Viking Age tragedy. *Inset left*: View of the sacred mountain of Slioch from Isle Maree. *Inset right*: Old coins hammered into the now dead money tree.

75. Mother Shipton's Cave

Knaresborough, North Yorkshire

Mother Shipton was England's most famous prophetess. She was born in a cave here in the 15th century and predicted many things which subsequently came true, such as the Spanish Armada, the English Civil War and the Great Fire of London.

Next to her cave is the famous Petrifying Well which quickly turns items to stone if they are left dangling under it.

Main: The Petrifying Well. Objects left dangling under it turn to stone in 3-5 months. *Inset*: Statue of Mother Shipton which has been recreated inside her cave.

76. St. Trillo's Chapel

Llandrillo-yn-Rhos, Conwy

St. Trillo was drawn to this spot in the 6th century by a column of light. Under the glowing column he found a sacred spring with magical healing properties.

Today this holy well can be found inside St. Trillo's Chapel, the smallest church in Wales!

Main: St. Trillo's Chapel lies by the seaside in Llandrillo-yn-rhos. *Inset*: The holy well sits under the altar inside the chapel.

77. Rough Tor

Bodmin Moor, Cornwall

Rough Tor is littered with prehistoric sites including stone circles, ancient settlements and burial cairns. There is a sacred spring emerging from the hillside and several huge Logan stones, magical 'rocking' stones that can weigh several tonnes each. Any woman who touches one of these logan stone nine times at midnight will become a witch!

Left main: Discovering the holy well on Rough Tor (Pronounced *Row*-ter). The well is aligned with the summer solstice sunset. *Left inset:* One of the stacks of strangely weathered stones balancing atop Rough Tor. *This page:* Natural water-filled depressions in the rock such as these are known as wart wells. Warts could be removed by sticking a pin in a wart and then placing the pin in the wart well. *Right*: A strangely weathered logan stone, one of the magical rocking stones of Rough Tor.

78. Tigh-nam-Bodach

Glen Lyon, Perthshire

Hidden away in Gleann Cailliche in the Scottish Highlands is the location of Britain's oldest pagan ritual. At Tigh-nam-Bodach every Beltain (1st May) curious stone statues are brought out from their small stone dwelling to watch over the valley for the coming summer. Then at Samhain (31st October) they are returned to their hut and sealed inside for the winter.

The Celtic crone goddess, the Cailleach, was once given shelter by the locals in this valley. In return she left these statues, representing her and her family, to watch over their cattle. Great misfortune will befall anyone who disturbs these statues

Main: The ancient river-worn statues of Tigh-nam-Bodach, brought out for the summer months to watch over the valley.

79. Men-An-Tol

Penwith Moors, Cornwall

Sitting high and lonely on the **P**enwith **M**oors, the holed stone of **M**en-**A**n-**T**ol has been known since ancient times for its magical cures.

Main: The holed stone at Men-an-Tol. *Below:* The three stones align to form a row.

Also known locally as the "**C**rick **S**tone" the holed stone at **M**en-an-**T**ol is said to cure pains in the neck and back, as well as rheumatism and scrofula. **C**hildren were passed through the hole in order to ensure good health, and the friendly pixie who inhabits the stone can return a changeling baby to its true human form.

Visitors may ask questions of the pixie by placing two pins in a cross shape in the groove on top of the stone and interpreting their movements.

80. Obtrush Roque

Also known as the hobgoblin's cairn, Obtrush Roque is located on a lonely windswept moor overlooking the valley of Farndale on the North York Moors.

County folklore 1899 relates the tale of a troublesome hob who once lived at the cairn and would make mischief for a local farmer. No longer able to take all his pranks the farmer packed his belongings in a cart, determined to leave the area for good.

"We're flitting!" the farmer said to his neighbour as he packed all his belongings on his cart. Then came a little voice from the butter churn: "Aye, we're flitting" said the hob!

Realising he would never be rid of the troublesome hob the farmer dejectedly unpacked his cart and returned home!

Main picture: Obtrush Roque. *Inset:* Memorials to Elphi the Farndale Hob at Ryedale Folk Museum, Hutton-Le-Hole.

Elphi the Farndale hob

"Elphi bandy-legs,
bent, an' wide apart,
No one in the dale
owns a kinder heart.
Elphi, great-head,
greatest ever seen,
No one in this dale
owns a brighter een.
Elphi, little chap,
thof he were so small,
Were big wi' deeds o' kindness,
drink to him one an' all.
Him at fails to drain dry,
be it mug or glass,
Binnot woth a pescod,
nor a buss frae onny lass."

This extract is from an old cookbook dated 1699. Elphi and his exploits were once well known in the local area.

Hobs are small shaggy household spirits similar to the Scottish brownie or the Scandinavian tomte. The county of Yorkshire abounds with tales of these strange beings who will help on the farm at nighttime for nothing more than a bowl of cream, but will be terribly upset if insulted and cause all kinds of mischief!

Directions to places of Magic and Miracles

71. Merlindale
Drumelzier, Scottish Borders

As you drive along the B712 from Drumelzier to Stobo you will see Tinnis Castle on your right - NT142344. Merlin's standing stone is directly North of Tinnis Castle by the river Tweed - NT139354. Merlin's alter stone is further up the valley opposite Altarstone Farm - NT157358

72. The Fairy Steps
Beetham, Cumbria

Follow the public footpath Southwest out of Beetham until you reach Whin Scar. After about 500m take the second public footpath to left which heads over the top of Whin Scar. When you reach the far side of Whin Scar you can then attempt to walk down the fairy steps - SD487789

73. Nevern Churchyard
Nevern, Pembrokeshire

St Brynach's church is in the middle of Nevern Village. The bleeding yew is the second tree on the right after you enter the gate - SN083400

74. Isle Maree
Loch Maree, Highland

Drive along the A832 which runs South of Loch Maree and stop at the Loch Maree Hotel in Talladale. There you can hire a boat to take you over to Isle Maree - NG931723

75. Mother Shipton's Cave
Knaresborough, North Yorkshire

Mother Shipton's Cave and the Petrifying Well sit by the river on the Western edge of Knaresborough. Park by the river and walk to the cave and well - SE346565 (entrance fee payable).

76. St. Trillo's Chapel
Llandrillo-yn-Rhos, Conwy

On the seafront just below Marine Drive on the Northeast corner of Llandrillo-yn-Rhos between College Avenue and Trillo Avenue. The chapel is locked but opens for Eucharist on Wednesdays. Check the timetable posted on the door - SH841811

77. Tigh-nam-Bodach
Pubil, Perth and Kinross

From Pubil take the track that leads along the North side of Loch Lyon. Continue on past the end of Loch Lyon, ignoring a left turn, and fording a small stream called the Allt Meurain. After another 1500m or so look for the small stone hut down by the river to your left - NN380426 (an 18km round trip).

78. Rough Tor
Camelford, Cornwall

Drive East out of Camelford until you reach the car park at the end of Roughtor Road. Climb the hillside ahead of you aiming between the two crags and look out for a faint gully to your left that hides the holy well. On right hand crag lies the logan stone - SX145807

79. Men-an-Tol
Morvah, Cornwall

Take the road from Morvah to Madron and after about 2km Men-an-Tol will be signposted down a track to your left. Park and then walk up the track for about 800m. Turn right down a public footpath and you will see Men-an-Tol ahead, about 100m away - SW426349

80. Obtrush Roque
Farndale, North Yorkshire

Park in Farndale near Low Mill then follow Mill Lane until it turns into a footpath leading up onto the moor. After passing through the woods take the path to the right and after about 400m turn left and strike directly South (uphill) for the cairn which sits atop the moor - SE662944

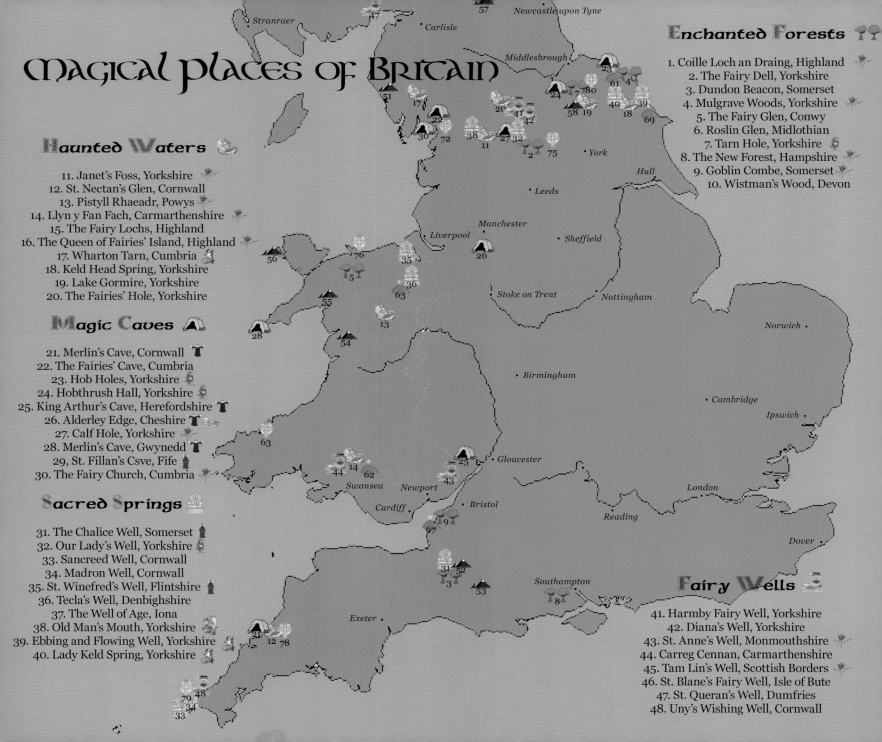

Magical Places of Britain

Haunted Waters

11. Janet's Foss, Yorkshire
12. St. Nectan's Glen, Cornwall
13. Pistyll Rhaeadr, Powys
14. Llyn y Fan Fach, Carmarthenshire
15. The Fairy Lochs, Highland
16. The Queen of Fairies' Island, Highland
17. Wharton Tarn, Cumbria
18. Keld Head Spring, Yorkshire
19. Lake Gormire, Yorkshire
20. The Fairies' Hole, Yorkshire

Magic Caves

21. Merlin's Cave, Cornwall
22. The Fairies' Cave, Cumbria
23. Hob Holes, Yorkshire
24. Hobthrush Hall, Yorkshire
25. King Arthur's Cave, Herefordshire
26. Alderley Edge, Cheshire
27. Calf Hole, Yorkshire
28. Merlin's Cave, Gwynedd
29. St. Fillan's Csve, Fife
30. The Fairy Church, Cumbria

Sacred Springs

31. The Chalice Well, Somerset
32. Our Lady's Well, Yorkshire
33. Sancreed Well, Cornwall
34. Madron Well, Cornwall
35. St. Winefred's Well, Flintshire
36. Tecla's Well, Denbighshire
37. The Well of Age, Iona
38. Old Man's Mouth, Yorkshire
39. Ebbing and Flowing Well, Yorkshire
40. Lady Keld Spring, Yorkshire

Enchanted Forests

1. Coille Loch an Draing, Highland
2. The Fairy Dell, Yorkshire
3. Dundon Beacon, Somerset
4. Mulgrave Woods, Yorkshire
5. The Fairy Glen, Conwy
6. Roslin Glen, Midlothian
7. Tarn Hole, Yorkshire
8. The New Forest, Hampshire
9. Goblin Combe, Somerset
10. Wistman's Wood, Devon

Fairy Wells

41. Harmby Fairy Well, Yorkshire
42. Diana's Well, Yorkshire
43. St. Anne's Well, Monmouthshire
44. Carreg Cennan, Carmarthenshire
45. Tam Lin's Well, Scottish Borders
46. St. Blane's Fairy Well, Isle of Bute
47. St. Queran's Well, Dumfries
48. Uny's Wishing Well, Cornwall

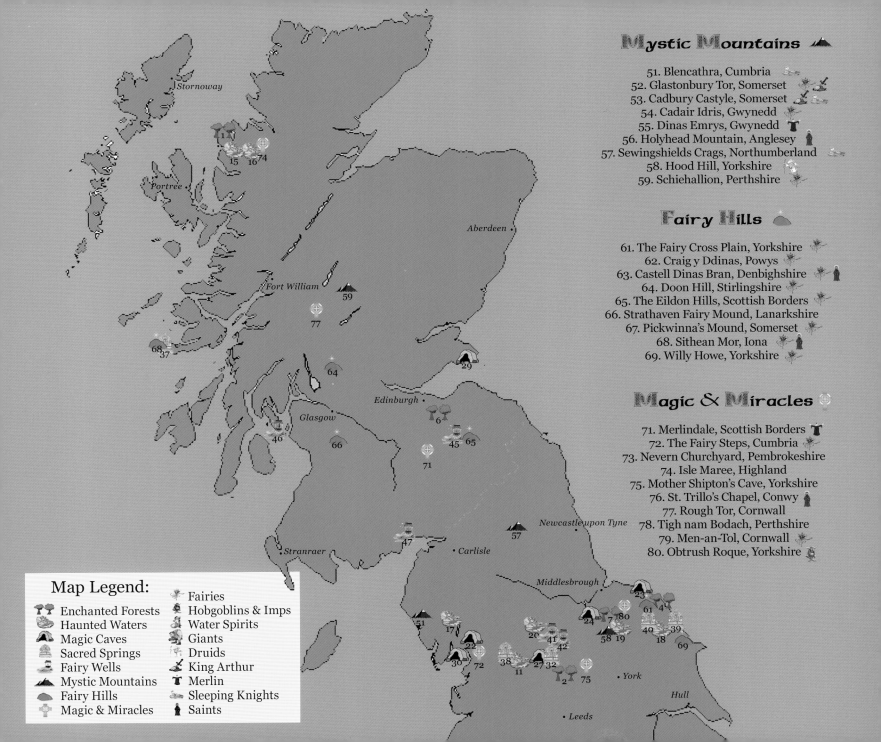

Mystic Mountains

51. Blencathra, Cumbria
52. Glastonbury Tor, Somerset
53. Cadbury Castyle, Somerset
54. Cadair Idris, Gwynedd
55. Dinas Emrys, Gwynedd
56. Holyhead Mountain, Anglesey
57. Sewingshields Crags, Northumberland
58. Hood Hill, Yorkshire
59. Schiehallion, Perthshire

Fairy Hills

61. The Fairy Cross Plain, Yorkshire
62. Craig y Ddinas, Powys
63. Castell Dinas Bran, Denbighshire
64. Doon Hill, Stirlingshire
65. The Eildon Hills, Scottish Borders
66. Strathaven Fairy Mound, Lanarkshire
67. Pickwinna's Mound, Somerset
68. Sithean Mor, Iona
69. Willy Howe, Yorkshire

Magic & Miracles

71. Merlindale, Scottish Borders
72. The Fairy Steps, Cumbria
73. Nevern Churchyard, Pembrokeshire
74. Isle Maree, Highland
75. Mother Shipton's Cave, Yorkshire
76. St. Trillo's Chapel, Conwy
77. Rough Tor, Cornwall
78. Tigh nam Bodach, Perthshire
79. Men-an-Tol, Cornwall
80. Obtrush Roque, Yorkshire

Map Legend:

- Enchanted Forests
- Haunted Waters
- Magic Caves
- Sacred Springs
- Fairy Wells
- Mystic Mountains
- Fairy Hills
- Magic & Miracles
- Fairies
- Hobgoblins & Imps
- Water Spirits
- Giants
- Druids
- King Arthur
- Merlin
- Sleeping Knights
- Saints

Showing Respect...

The Magical Places in this book are sacred sites that deserve to be treated with respect. You may feel compelled to leave a small offering of food, flowers or some other bio-degradable object that you have hand-crafted yourself. It is best pause and silently ask permission before entering, and when you do so you should enter quietly and respectfully.

It's best not to leave any modern items, plastic or rubbish, and if you must tie clooties (i.e. rags & ribbons) then make sure they are made from 100% natural materials (e.g. wool, linen, silk). Clooties were normally tied in special locations in order to cure diseases. As the rag rotted away so the disease or malady would disappear. If there is any plastic or man-made fibers in your clootie then it will never rot away. Too many clooties make an eyesore.

It was a common custom in ancient times to leave offerings of coins or other items in sacred springs, but please be aware that whereas silver has the property of purify water, modern coins and other items will only pollute the waters.

These places have been sacred sites since ancient times. Our ancestors long ago in the pagan past could make direct contact with the spirits here. If you treat the place with respect and leave behind all the preconceptions of the modern world then you too may also be able to lift the veil and see into the otherworld of spirits.

When you enter a sacred site take some time to sit down, eyes closed and take some deep breaths. Sit silently for a while and see what impressions you can pick up from the place and if you can detect any presence there. After a while open your eyes and view the place in a new light, you may notice something that you were not aware of before. If you're lucky then with patience you might just catch a glimpse of the fairies or other magical beings that reside there!

Good luck and I wish you many magical adventures!

Above: A simple offering left at Uny's Wishing Well, Carbis Bay, Cornwall

About the Author

Rob Wildwood is a practicing pagan and amateur photographer from Yorkshire in the North of England.

He has been visiting magical places all his life and he writes a blog called 'The Land of the Fae' where he talks about his spiritual experiences at these sacred sites -
www.landofthefae.com

This book is the result of three years research into Britain's ancient folklore and a fascination for the magical beings which once inhabited our sacred landscape.

Rob's interest in primitive beliefs has led him to spend time with tribal people including the Bushmen of the Kalahari, the Penan of Borneo and the Naikas of Southwest India, inquiring about their ancient knowledge of the world of spirits and the sacred sites that these spirits inhabit.

He was then inspired to return home and travel extensively around the British Isles hunting out these forgotten places of magic and mystery in his own land.

Not all the places visited have been included in this book and there are certainly many more out there just waiting to be discovered!

Rob is currently based in sacred Glastonbury in Somerset where he studies shamanism and attends the occasional faery ball (see photo!) He also manages a successful online business selling historical handmade crafts -
www.jelldragon.com

He has recently created his own publishing company called Wyldwood Publishing and this book is its first publication.